Your Photo Here

THIS PASSPORT BELONGS TO:

CHEF _____

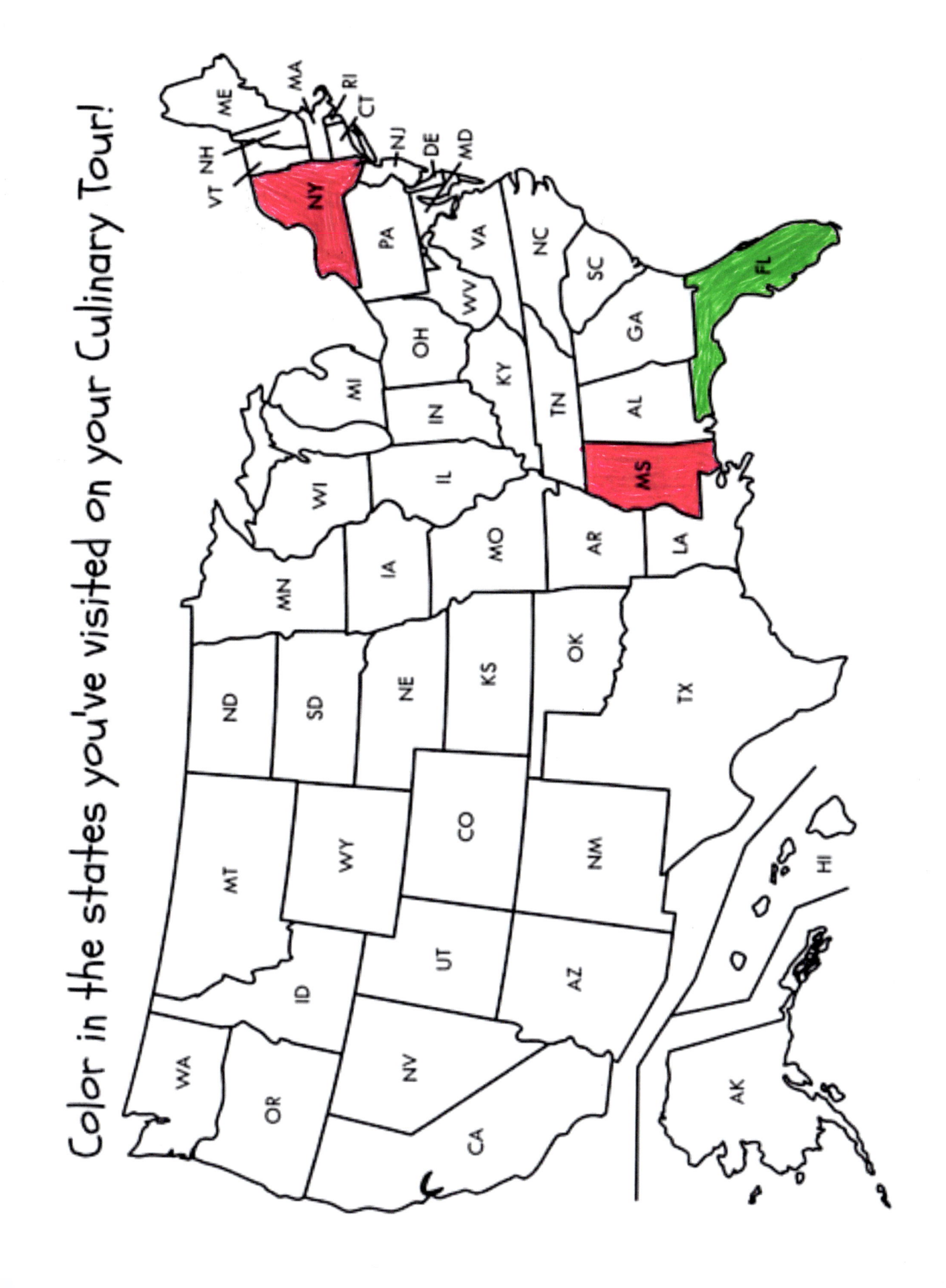

Color in the states you've visited on your Culinary Tour!

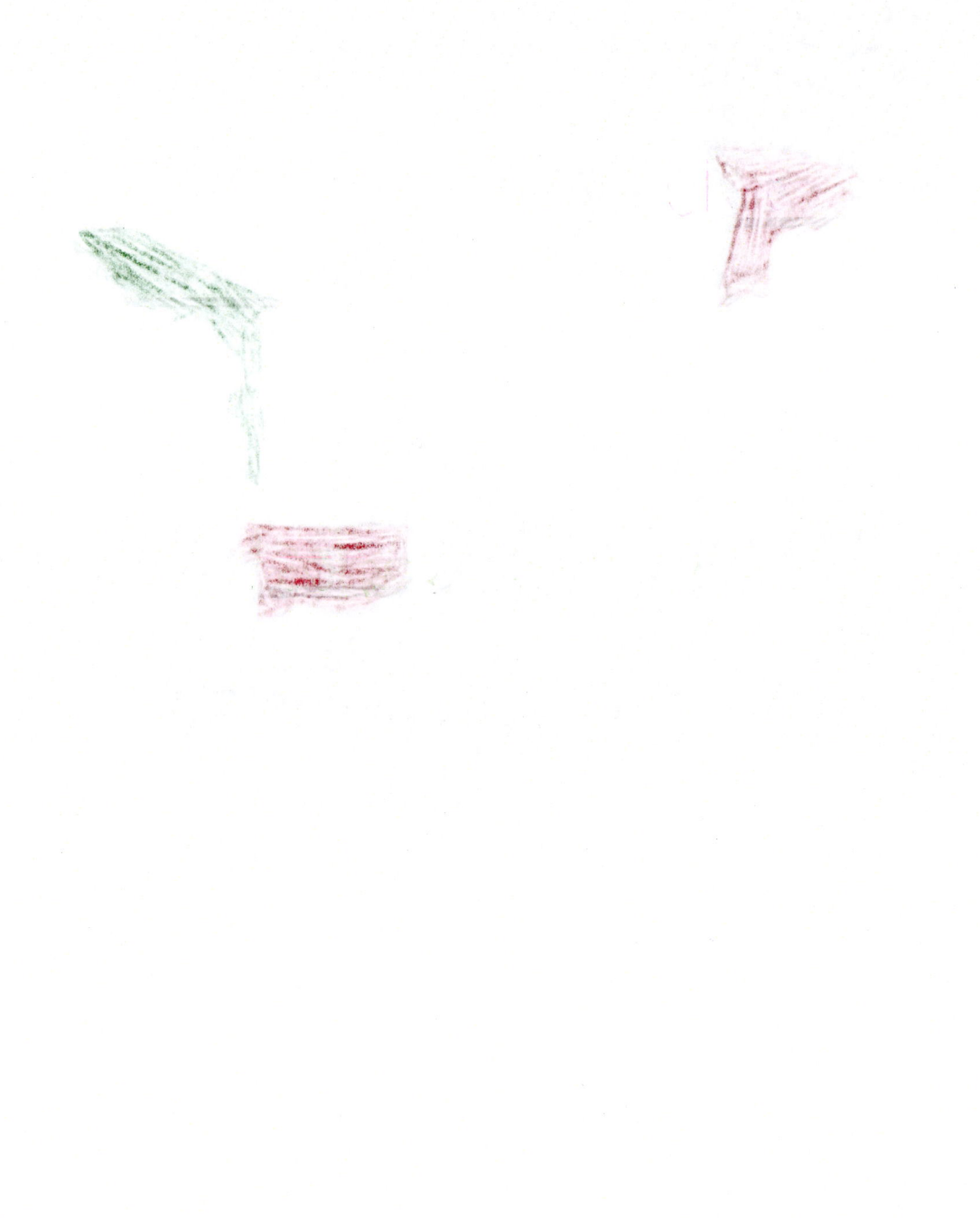

Place: New york

Recipe: bagles

What Did I Learn?

I learned how to make bagles! Next time I'll get fresh yeast, and check the temp. of o.

- [✓] Tried It!
- [✓] Yum!
- [ ] Yuck!

Place: Florida

Recipe: Key-lime cheesecake

What Did I Learn?

I learned how to make cheesecake!

- [✓] Tried It!
- [✓] Yum!
- [ ] Yuck!

Place: __Mississippi__

Recipe: __Mississippi mud pie__

What Did I Learn?

__to make cupcakes__

☑ Tried It!   ☑ Yum!   ☐ Yuck!

Place: _____

Recipe: _____
_____

What Did I Learn?

_____
_____
_____
_____
_____

☐ Tried It!   ☐ Yum!   ☐ Yuck!

Place: _____

Recipe: _____
_____

What Did I Learn?

_____
_____
_____
_____
_____
_____

☐ Tried It!   ☐ Yum!   ☐ Yuck!

Place: _____

Recipe: _____
_____

What Did I Learn?

_____
_____
_____
_____
_____

Tried It!   Yum!   Yuck!

Place: _____

Recipe: _____
_____

What Did I Learn?

_____
_____
_____
_____
_____
_____

☐ Tried It!   ☐ Yum!   ☐ Yuck!

Place: _____

Recipe: _____
_____

What Did I Learn?
_____
_____
_____
_____
_____
_____

☐ Tried It! ☐ Yum! ☐ Yuck!

Place: _____

Recipe: _____
_____

What Did I Learn?

_____
_____
_____
_____
_____
_____

☐ Tried It!   ☐ Yum!   ☐ Yuck!

Place: _____

Recipe: _____
_____

What Did I Learn?

_____
_____
_____
_____
_____

☐ Tried It!   ☐ Yum!   ☐ Yuck!

Place: _____

Recipe: _____
_____

What Did I Learn?

_____
_____
_____
_____
_____
_____
_____

☐ Tried It!   ☐ Yum!   ☐ Yuck!

Place: _____

Recipe: _____
_____

What Did I Learn?

_____
_____
_____
_____
_____
_____

☐ Tried It!   ☐ Yum!   ☐ Yuck!

Place: _____

Recipe: _____
_____

What Did I Learn?

_____
_____
_____
_____
_____
_____
_____

☐ Tried It!   ☐ Yum!   ☐ Yuck!

Place: _____

Recipe: _____
_____

What Did I Learn?

_____
_____
_____
_____
_____
_____

☐ Tried It!   ☐ Yum!   ☐ Yuck!

Place: _____

Recipe: _____
_____

What Did I Learn?

_____
_____
_____
_____
_____
_____

☐ Tried It!   ☐ Yum!   ☐ Yuck!

Place: _____

Recipe: _____
_____

What Did I Learn?

_____
_____
_____
_____
_____
_____

☐ Tried It!   ☐ Yum!   ☐ Yuck!

Place: _____

Recipe: _____
_____

What Did I Learn?

_____
_____
_____
_____
_____
_____

☐ Tried It!   ☐ Yum!   ☐ Yuck!

Place: _____

Recipe: _____
_____

What Did I Learn?

_____
_____
_____
_____
_____

☐ Tried It!   ☐ Yum!   ☐ Yuck!

Place: _____

Recipe: _____
_____

What Did I Learn?

_____
_____
_____
_____
_____
_____

☐ Tried It!   ☐ Yum!   ☐ Yuck!

Place: _____

Recipe: _____
_____

What Did I Learn?

_____
_____
_____
_____
_____
_____

☐ Tried It!   ☐ Yum!   ☐ Yuck!

Place: _____

Recipe: _____
_____

What Did I Learn?

_____
_____
_____
_____
_____
_____
_____

Tried It!   Yum!   Yuck!

Place: _____

Recipe: _____
_____

What Did I Learn?

_____
_____
_____
_____
_____
_____

☐ Tried It!   ☐ Yum!   ☐ Yuck!

Place: _____

Recipe: _____
_____

What Did I Learn?

_____
_____
_____
_____
_____
_____

☐ Tried It! ☐ Yum! ☐ Yuck!

Place: _____

Recipe: _____
_____

What Did I Learn?

_____
_____
_____
_____
_____
_____

Tried It!   Yum!   Yuck!

Place: _____

Recipe: _____
_____

What Did I Learn?

_____
_____
_____
_____
_____
_____

☐ Tried It! ☐ Yum! ☐ Yuck!

Place: _____

Recipe: _____
_____

What Did I Learn?

_____
_____
_____
_____
_____
_____

☐ Tried It!   ☐ Yum!   ☐ Yuck!

Place: _____

Recipe: _____
_____

What Did I Learn?

_____
_____
_____
_____
_____
_____

☐ Tried It!   ☐ Yum!   ☐ Yuck!

Place: _____

Recipe: _____
_____

What Did I Learn?

_____
_____
_____
_____
_____
_____

☐ Tried It!   ☐ Yum!   ☐ Yuck!

Place: _____

Recipe: _____
_____

What Did I Learn?

_____
_____
_____
_____
_____
_____

☐ Tried It!   ☐ Yum!   ☐ Yuck!

Place: _____

Recipe: _____
_____

What Did I Learn?

_____
_____
_____
_____
_____

☐ Tried It!   ☐ Yum!   ☐ Yuck!

Place: _____

Recipe: _____
_____

What Did I Learn?

_____
_____
_____
_____
_____
_____

☐ Tried It!   ☐ Yum!   ☐ Yuck!

Place: _____

Recipe: _____
_____

What Did I Learn?

_____
_____
_____
_____
_____
_____

Tried It!   Yum!   Yuck!

Place: _____

Recipe: _____
_____

What Did I Learn?

_____
_____
_____
_____
_____
_____

☐ Tried It!   ☐ Yum!   ☐ Yuck!

Place: _____

Recipe: _____
_____

What Did I Learn?

_____
_____
_____
_____
_____
_____

Tried It!   Yum!   Yuck!

Place: _____

Recipe: _____
_____

What Did I Learn?

_____
_____
_____
_____
_____
_____

☐ Tried It!   ☐ Yum!   ☐ Yuck!

Place: _____

Recipe: _____
_____

What Did I Learn?

_____
_____
_____
_____
_____

☐ Tried It!   ☐ Yum!   ☐ Yuck!

Place: _____

Recipe: _____
_____

What Did I Learn?

_____
_____
_____
_____
_____
_____

☐ Tried It!   ☐ Yum!   ☐ Yuck!

Place: _____

Recipe: _____
_____

What Did I Learn?

_____
_____
_____
_____
_____
_____

☐ Tried It!   ☐ Yum!   ☐ Yuck!

Place: _____

Recipe: _____
_____

What Did I Learn?

_____
_____
_____
_____
_____
_____

Tried It!   Yum!   Yuck!

Place: _____

Recipe: _____
_____

What Did I Learn?

_____
_____
_____
_____
_____

Tried It!   Yum!   Yuck!

Place: _____

Recipe: _____
_____

What Did I Learn?
_____
_____
_____
_____
_____
_____
_____

☐ Tried It!   ☐ Yum!   ☐ Yuck!

Place: _____

Recipe: _____
_____

What Did I Learn?

_____
_____
_____
_____
_____

☐ Tried It!   ☐ Yum!   ☐ Yuck!

Place: _____

Recipe: _____
_____

What Did I Learn?

_____
_____
_____
_____
_____
_____

☐ Tried It!   ☐ Yum!   ☐ Yuck!

Place: _____

Recipe: _____
_____

What Did I Learn?

_____
_____
_____
_____
_____
_____

Tried It!   Yum!   Yuck!

Place: _____

Recipe: _____
_____

What Did I Learn?

_____
_____
_____
_____
_____
_____

☐ Tried It!   ☐ Yum!   ☐ Yuck!

Place: _____

Recipe: _____
_____

What Did I Learn?

_____
_____
_____
_____
_____
_____

Tried It! Yum! Yuck!

Place: _____

Recipe: _____
_____

What Did I Learn?

_____
_____
_____
_____
_____
_____
_____

☐ Tried It!   ☐ Yum!   ☐ Yuck!

Place: _____

Recipe: _____
_____

What Did I Learn?

_____
_____
_____
_____
_____
_____

☐ Tried It!   ☐ Yum!   ☐ Yuck!

Place: _____

Recipe: _____
_____

What Did I Learn?

_____
_____
_____
_____
_____
_____

☐ Tried It!   ☐ Yum!   ☐ Yuck!

Place: _____

Recipe: _____
_____

What Did I Learn?

_____
_____
_____
_____
_____
_____

☐ Tried It!   ☐ Yum!   ☐ Yuck!

Place: _____

Recipe: _____
_____

What Did I Learn?

_____
_____
_____
_____
_____
_____

☐ Tried It!   ☐ Yum!   ☐ Yuck!

Place: _____

Recipe: _____
_____

What Did I Learn?

_____
_____
_____
_____
_____
_____

☐ Tried It!   ☐ Yum!   ☐ Yuck!

Place: _____

Recipe: _____
_____

What Did I Learn?

_____
_____
_____
_____
_____
_____

☐ Tried It! ☐ Yum! ☐ Yuck!

Place: _____

Recipe: _____
_____

What Did I Learn?
_____
_____
_____
_____
_____
_____

☐ Tried It!   ☐ Yum!   ☐ Yuck!

Place: _____

Recipe: _____
_____

What Did I Learn?

_____
_____
_____
_____
_____
_____

☐ Tried It!   ☐ Yum!   ☐ Yuck!

Place: _____

Recipe: _____
_____

What Did I Learn?

_____
_____
_____
_____
_____
_____

☐ Tried It!   ☐ Yum!   ☐ Yuck!

Place: _____

Recipe: _____
_____

What Did I Learn?

_____
_____
_____
_____
_____
_____

☐ Tried It! ☐ Yum! ☐ Yuck!

Place: _____

Recipe: _____
_____

What Did I Learn?

_____
_____
_____
_____
_____
_____

☐ Tried It!   ☐ Yum!   ☐ Yuck!

Place: _____

Recipe: _____
_____

What Did I Learn?

_____
_____
_____
_____
_____
_____

☐ Tried It!   ☐ Yum!   ☐ Yuck!

Place: _____

Recipe: _____
_____

What Did I Learn?

_____
_____
_____
_____
_____

☐ Tried It!   ☐ Yum!   ☐ Yuck!

Place: _____

Recipe: _____
_____

What Did I Learn?

_____
_____
_____
_____
_____
_____

☐ Tried It!   ☐ Yum!   ☐ Yuck!

Place: _____

Recipe: _____
_____

What Did I Learn?

_____
_____
_____
_____
_____
_____

☐ Tried It!   ☐ Yum!   ☐ Yuck!

Place: _____

Recipe: _____
_____

What Did I Learn?

_____
_____
_____
_____
_____
_____

Tried It!   Yum!   Yuck!

Place: _____

Recipe: _____
_____

What Did I Learn?
_____
_____
_____
_____
_____
_____

☐ Tried It!   ☐ Yum!   ☐ Yuck!

Place: _____

Recipe: _____
_____

What Did I Learn?

_____
_____
_____
_____
_____
_____

☐ Tried It! ☐ Yum! ☐ Yuck!

a lovin' spoonful

www.alovinspoonful.net

Visit our website to join us on our culinary adventure and find recipes to start your own Kids Culinary Tour!

©2016 Alovinspoonful.net

Cardamom Rice Pudding & Roasted Plums

Crumble:
- 1/2 C Flour
- 1/4 C light brown sugar
- 1/4 C white sugar
- 1/4 C slivered almonds
- 1 tsp cinnamon
- 1/4 tsp salt
- 4 Tbsp unsalted butter, melted

Mash together with your fingers. Spread it out on a lightly greased parchment lined baking sheet.

Bake in a 350° oven for 8-10 min. Remove from oven & cool.

Pudding:
- 1 C water
- 1/4 tsp salt
- 1 Tbsp unsalted butter
- 1/2 C Arborio rice
- 2 C milk
- 4 Tbsp sugar
- 1 tsp vanilla
- 1/4 tsp Cardamom
- 1/4 tsp Cinnamon

Add water, rice, salt & butter to medium sauce pan. Bring to a boil. Reduce heat, cover, simmer 15 min. Rice al dente.

In a large saucepan, simmer remaining ingredients, stirring frequently.

When rice is done, stir it into the milk & simmer 15 min. Transfer to a bowl & cool.

Place sliced in baking dish & sprinkle with brown sugar. Put pats of butter on top and bake 15 m at 375.

1-2 plums sliced into 8ths, 1/4 C brown sugar, 3 Tbsp unsalted butter